THE GREEK GIFT TO THE WORLD

'**B**eware the Greeks bearing gifts,' wailed Cassandra, as the wooden horse was dragged into the city of Troy. The story of the wooden horse is just one of many left by the ancient Greeks. But they left much more than a rich heritage of stories, myths and legends. They laid many of the foundation stones on which Western civilization was built: foundations of art, architecture, law, science, mathematics, philosophy, technology and sport that underpin much of global culture today.

Some 3,000 years ago, the Greeks were a mixture of peoples, united by some common beliefs, language and a way of life based on farming, fishing, seagoing trade and small, vibrant cities. Their culture had distinct local flavours, wherever it evolved: in Crete, Mycenae, Athens, Sparta, Thebes and Corinth, and in many islands and colonies from the Black Sea to the western Mediterranean. This culture produced figures of immense intellectual stature: Plato, Aristotle, Aeschylus, Archimedes, to name but four. To later generations, these figures seemed even more impressive than the gods of Mount Olympus.

Equally significant was the Greek gift to political theory: democracy. The Greeks created the city-state, or *polis*, each with its own system of government. Athens, the richest and largest, nurtured the fledgling democracy. The Greek city-states maintained a spirited, often quarrelsome, independence, and they united only when they were threatened by a common enemy, Persia. In the end the city-states were unified by a king with dreams of an empire greater even than that of Persia: Alexander the Great of Macedonia.

In terms of world history, the 'Greek period' lasted from about 3000 BC to the beginning of the Roman Empire. The Classical period, the most celebrated phase of the ancient Greek civilization, lasted from about 480 BC to 336 BC. This was a time of particularly diverse achievement, when Greeks generated ideas about government, philosophy, science, sport and art that altered the way of the world.

Stater (coin) of Philip II, king of Macedonia and father of Alexander the Great. The stater depicts the Greek sun god, Apollo.

Four caryatids (female figures acting as columns) on the porch of the Erectheum, on the Acropolis in Athens. The temple was built between 421 and 407 BC.

A warrior from the sea. Made between 460 and 430 BC, this 'Riace bronze' statue was one of two lost at sea in ancient times (perhaps while being shipped to Rome) and was salvaged off the coast of Riace, Italy, in 1972. Even without his shield and spear, he still cuts a formidable figure.

Minoan and Mycenean Greece

The Athenians and other mainland Greeks shared a history and culture with islanders of the Aegean Sea, such as the peoples of the Cyclades (Kos, Naxos and surrounding islands) and the island of Crete. While mainland Greeks, 5,000 years ago, were living as hunters, farmers and herders of goats and sheep, the Cretans built a rich civilization with, from around 2000 BC, splendid royal palaces. Artistic and peaceable, skilled as painters and metalworkers, the Cretans were also traders. Wall paintings in Egypt show Cretan envoys offering gifts to the pharaoh, and acrobats vaulting over bulls – a Cretan speciality.

The Cretan civilization is known as 'Minoan', after the Cretan king Minos. Aegean high culture flourished until around 1450 BC, when the Cretan palaces were destroyed by fire. The Palace of Knossos survived perhaps another 150 years, until it was also destroyed. These calamities appear to have happened after the island volcano of Thera (Santorini) blew its top between 1600 and 1500 BC, with seismic effects on the Aegean status quo. Debris and possibly a tsunami struck Crete, causing many people to flee the island.

Leaping monkeys, a wall decoration in a house on the island of Thera (Santorini), north of Crete. Minoan houses were decorated with scenes of animals, everyday life and military activities.

A gold pendant from Minoan Crete. The wild mountain goat was a favourite subject for Minoan art. The pendant dates from between 1700 and 1550 BC and is now in the British Museum.

The Lion Gate at Mycenae in Greece. Mycenean royal palaces were protected by enormous stone walls, up to 9 metres (30 feet) high.

ISLAND OF THE MINOTAUR

King Minos of Crete was punished by the god Poseidon after the king kept for himself a white bull, given by Poseidon for sacrifice. His queen, Pasiphae, conceived a passion for the bull, and gave birth to the Minotaur. Half-man and half-bull, this monster lived in the Labyrinth, devouring human victims, until slain by the Athenian hero Theseus, with the help of Minos' daughter Ariadne.

The Myceneans, a people living in the Peloponnese (the southern peninsula of mainland Greece), had begun to play a part in Cretan affairs before the collapse of the Minoan civilization. After the fall of Knossos, the Myceneans became the most powerful people in the Aegean. Mycenean kings were warriors rather than traders. Their stone fortresses, such as Tiryns, were so massive that later Greeks thought the huge stones must be the work of giants.

On the eastern side of the Aegean Sea was Troy (Ilium). Its war with the Greeks inspired one of the greatest stories in world literature, a poetic epic composed in the 700s BC and traditionally ascribed to Homer. The *Iliad* begins with the abduction of Helen, wife of King Menelaus of Sparta, by Paris, son of King Priam of Troy. With his brother, Agamemnon of Mycenae, Menelaus set sail to get Helen back. After a war lasting 10 years, the Greeks tricked their way into Troy by hiding soldiers inside a wooden horse. Troy was destroyed. Troy was a real city in what is now northwest Turkey. In the 1870s German archaeologist Heinrich Schliemann excavated the area, and later archaeologists revealed the remains of several cities. The site known today as Troy VIIa is most often identified with the Troy that was burned by the Greeks.

Reconstruction of the throne room of the Palace of Knossos, c.1500 BC, painted by Edwin J. Lambert (fl.1877–1928).

THE GREEK WAY

With the end of the Mycenean civilization (for reasons still unclear) around 1100 BC, Greece entered a period known as the Dark Age, when Greek culture declined. The period lasted until about 800 BC, when the Greeks began to spread across the sea in search of new land. Already skilled at trading in the Aegean, they began to found colonies, for example on islands such as Euboea and Naxos and on the coast of Asia Minor. Their ships also journeyed west to Italy (where colonies were founded at Naples and Syracuse) and to France, where they settled at Marseille. The Greeks had become, in their own words, like 'frogs sitting around a pond'.

Through contact with another seafaring people, the Phoenicians, the Greeks developed an alphabet. Written records on pottery began in this period, from which the Greeks dated their own history, starting with the first Olympic Games in 776 BC.

A ceramic perfume bottle made in the shape of a sandalled foot, from the colony of Taras (Taranto) in Italy and dating from the 7th century BC.

A relief showing an Athenian youth greeting an older man; from the 5th century BC.

A woman kneading dough to make bread on a slab of stone, c.500– 475 BC. It comes from Aulis, the port in Boeotia which by tradition was the embarkation point for the Greek fleet that sailed to attack Troy.

Colonist or stay-at-home, most Greeks were farmers, herders or fishermen. Not all were free – a poor farmer might be forced into slavery if he got into debt or lost his land to a richer neighbour. The landless and those with specialist skills (potters, armourers, masons, carpenters, metal-workers, lawyers, artists) clustered together in small cities, which evolved into city-states. The city became the centre of public and commercial life. In Athens, foreigners could do business in the city, but might not become citizens. Craftsmen, such as metalworkers, sandal-makers and potters, plied their trades in small workshops. Painted pottery, even when in fragments, has helped reveal glimpses of what life was like.

Houses were built close together. Many people had no separate kitchen and often bought cooked food from stalls and cafés. Men were more numerous on the streets than women, at least in Athens, where well-to-do men did the family shopping, accompanied by a slave, while their wives stayed at home. Poor women mingled more freely with men, for their work included fetching water from wells and springs in pottery jars and goat-skin bags. The streets were lively and noisy, but odorous, since there were no drains. Slaves were very prominent: out of a population of no more than 250,000 to 300,000 in Athens, between a quarter and a third were slaves.

GREEK VOYAGERS

According to legend, Marseille (Massilia) was founded in 600 BC by Phocaeans (Greeks from Asia Minor). They landed just as the local chief was about to offer his daughter in marriage to a group of warriors. When she saw the Greeks, she chose one of them instead. In the 4th century BC, Pytheas sailed from Massilia to navigate around 'the Island of Tin' (Britain).

CRADLE OF DEMOCRACY

Athens sat on the Attic plain surrounded by hills, with the port of Piraeus serving as its lifeline to the sea. The original site was the Acropolis ('high city'), possibly once a Mycenean stronghold. Athenian legend ascribed the building of the city to the hero Theseus.

Having ejected its last king in 683 BC, Athens became an aristocratic republic, ruled by elected magistrates or archons (at first three, later nine), who served a year-long term, after which they were elevated to the Areopagus, an Athenian equivalent to a combined US Supreme Court and Senate. Democracy began to take root with the reforms of the archon Solon.

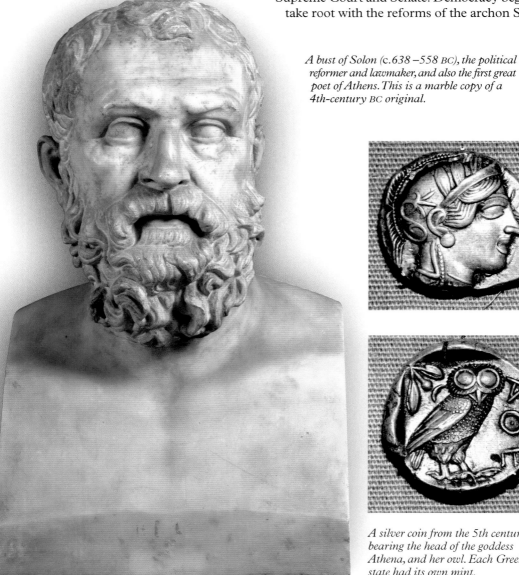

A bust of Solon (c.638 –558 BC), the political reformer and lawmaker, and also the first great poet of Athens. This is a marble copy of a 4th-century BC original.

A silver coin from the 5th century BC bearing the head of the goddess Athena, and her owl. Each Greek city-state had its own mint.

OSTRACISM

In Athens, from 487 BC to about 416 BC, citizens voted once a year on the question, 'Is there a potential tyrant here?' By 'tyrant' they meant a dictator – not necessarily malevolent, but all-powerful. Voters returned two months later with pieces of broken pottery (*ostraka*), on which they had scratched the name of the politician they most disliked or feared. He who had the most votes was exiled, or ostracized, for 10 years.

A pottery fragment or ostrakon *bearing the name of Themistocles (524–460 BC), who was ostracized from Athens in 472 BC.*

A view of Athens, showing the Parthenon on the Acropolis overlooking the city.

With fields and olive groves being acquired by a land-grabbing nobility, many poor Athenian peasant-farmers fell into debt and were forced to become slaves. Solon ended the practice of debt slavery and enfranchised anyone, regardless of birth, who met a certain wealth-qualification. He introduced an elected council of 400 and an assembly that voted on matters brought to it by the council. He also encouraged trade within Attica, the region surrounding Athens, to help the economy grow. But the poor were still ready to trust in one man. Peisistratus, who seized power and ruled as tyrant of Athens from about 560 to 527 BC, was popular because he took land from his rich enemies and redistributed it. He was succeeded by his son Hippias who also ruled as tyrant, until he was ousted in 510 BC.

After the overthrow of the tyranny, the reformer Cleisthenes gave democracy fresh impetus. He brought in a constitution, unwritten but observed for hundreds of years thereafter. It granted voting rights on the council to all free adult males and divided citizens into 10 tribes from all over Attica, shifting power away from the old aristocratic clans. The council was reorganized so it had 500 members: 50 from each tribe, chosen by drawing lots. The council proposed laws to the assembled citizens. This was the germ of democracy, but women were excluded, since they were not regarded as citizens.

WARRIOR KINGDOM

Sparta, Athens' main rival, is said to have been taken over during the Dark Age by Dorian invaders from the north. They made it a militarist state, reduced the native Spartans to serfdom (as helots) and later subjugated weaker neighbours such as the Messenians.

While Athens experimented with forms of democracy, Sparta retained its kings – in fact, the Spartans had two kings at the same time. They attributed their institutions to Lycurgus the law-giver, who may or may not have been an actual historical figure. Sparta's government was in effect an oligarchy (governed by a small group of people): it was ruled by a council of 28 elders, including the two kings, and an assembly in which men aged 30 or above met and voted by loud shouts. Having two kings meant that one could maintain order at home, while the other went to war.

Many Spartan women were as physical as the men; this bronze statuette dating from the 6th century BC shows a female athlete.

The remains of the theatre at the ancient capital of Sparta. According to legend, Sparta was founded by Lacedaemon, who named the city Sparta after his wife.

A bronze statuette of a Spartan soldier. His crested helmet made him look even more intimidating as he advanced, with spear and shield, on the enemy.

SPARTAN VALUES

According to legend, when a Spartan mother sent her son off to battle, she would tell him 'Come back with your shield, or on it.' To come back without his shield meant he had laid it down and broken ranks, so was guilty of cowardice. To return on his shield was to be carried home, either wounded or dead. Despite the grim reputation of the Spartans, their virtues were admired. The historian Plutarch (c.AD 46–120) relates how an old man looked in vain for an empty seat at the Olympic Games. Only the Spartans rose, almost as one, to offer him a place – proving the point that 'all Greeks know what is right, but only the Spartans do it.'

At the age of 20, every male citizen of Sparta became a soldier. Sparta had the only full-time army in Greece, so it was militarily stronger than any other city-state, including Athens, whose men only fought when their farm crops had been safely gathered in. Spartan citizens spent their time hunting, exercising, training for battle, living in barracks most of the time and eating food that other Greeks scornfully considered to be awful.

Every Spartan citizen received a portion of land, but he was not supposed to engage in commerce or waste time building a fancy home and his farm was worked by his wife and his helots. Wealth and material possessions were regarded with distaste, as were coins – Spartans used iron bars as currency.

Spartan child-rearing was rigorous: weak infants were left to die; boys left home at the age of seven to go to school, where the emphasis was on physical training and discipline. Both boys and girls did strenuous exercise and took part in sports.

This marble relief shows a Spartan princess – Philis, the daughter of King Cleomenes (died c.219 BC). Spartan women had more freedom than most Greek women.

9

GREEKS AT WAR

Sparta and Athens were never natural allies, but they fought together against the Persian Empire, whose kings regarded all Greeks, whether living within the empire (Asiatic Greeks) or outside (Ionic Greeks), as subject peoples. In 490 BC, the Persian king Darius launched a massive show of strength and invaded Greece. The Persian Wars, which lasted on and off from 490 to 449 BC, provided some of the epic events of Greek history.

The Greeks met Darius' invading army at Marathon. Spartans took no part in this battle – their reason being religious: they had first to observe a full-Moon festival. Marathon was a famous Greek victory. Pheidippides, a Greek soldier, ran 240 kilometres (150 miles) to fetch help, fought in the Battle of Marathon, then ran 42 kilometres (26 miles) back to Athens with news of the victory. He died, gasping 'Rejoice, we conquer!' His epic run is commemorated in the modern marathon race.

A Greek helmet with cheek and nose plates. To make such a helmet, in sheet bronze, required great skill on the part of the armourer.

Persian warriors, on a brick wall in the royal palace at Susa (Iran). Modern research suggests that the Persian army at Marathon probably numbered around 60,000, perhaps five times greater than the Greek army.

THE TRIREME

Athens was the supreme naval power in the Aegean Sea. Its main battleship was the trireme. This was a heavy galley with three banks of oars. In battle, it was driven at speed to ram the enemy by its oarsmen (170 men, all trained citizens). On deck were 30 soldiers, ready for hand-to-hand fighting. Triremes could disable an enemy ship by running alongside and smashing its oars.

Olympias, a reconstruction of an Athenian trireme, built 1985–87 in Piraeus, Greece. The ram cut through the water with 36.5 metres (120 feet) of solidly crafted muscle behind it.

The Persians returned in 480 BC with a much bigger army. Xerxes, son of Darius, led an army said by the Greek historian Herodotus to number over 5 million. Such a vast number may not be credible but the Greeks were certainly far out-numbered. The Spartan ethic was epitomized by their king Leonidas, who died heroically with 300 Spartan citizens (part of a combined Greek force totalling around 4,000) in a three-day defence of the pass at Thermopylae against the Persian army. The Persians captured Athens and laid waste to the temples on the Acropolis. Told by the Oracle at Delphi to 'trust in wooden walls', the Greeks now put their faith in their ships. Athens provided the core of the fleet of 350 warships that barred the way to the Persian fleet.

The battle fought at Salamis, an Aegean island in the Saronic Gulf, west of Piraeus, was the first major naval battle in history. The Persian fleet of around 800 ships easily outnumbered that of the Greeks. Themistocles, the Greek commander, withdrew into the narrow strait at Salamis, where the Persian ships, in pursuit, found themselves unable to manoeuvre. The Greek triremes then drove amongst them. Up to 300 Persian ships were sunk or burned, the Greeks losing only 40. The survivors of the Persian fleet scattered. Salamis gave the Greeks time to unite their armies on land. The Spartans were now in the field and their soldiers completed the Greeks' victory at the Battle of Plataea in 479 BC.

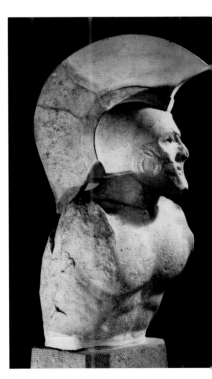

Head of Leonidas, the Spartan king who led his men in the heroic defence of the narrow pass at Thermopylae in 480 BC. The bust dates from 190 BC.

THE GOLDEN AGE IN ATHENS

The Parthenon has eight Doric columns along the front – six was more usual. The building was a temple to Athena and a city treasury. It housed a giant statue of the goddess over 9 metres (30 feet) tall, made of gold and ivory.

This red-figure vase, depicting a warrior returning home from war, was made between 475 and 450 BC.

After the Persian wars, thousands of oarsmen, victors at Salamis and holding the key to Athenian dominance in the Aegean, demanded more political power in Athens. This resulted in a tussle between the 'democrats' and the 'conservatives', the small group of rich noblemen who had previously controlled military and civic affairs.

Pericles (*c*.495–429 BC) led Athens at the height of its power. Leader of the democratic party, he gained popular support as a military commander in the 440s BC against Euboea and Samos. From 440 to 432 BC, he set about transforming Athens. A vast building programme was undertaken to restore the Acropolis, with new marble temples reached by a monumental gateway, the Propylaia. At the heart of the new Acropolis was the Parthenon, a temple erected in honour of the city's patron goddess, Athena. The Erectheum, built between 421 and 407 BC, was a particularly sacred building, associated with at least eight deities. A third, smaller, temple on the Acropolis was dedicated to Athena Nike.

Under Pericles, citizens were paid for the first time for sitting as councillors and jurymen – so encouraging the participation of poorer men. Trade goods filled the warehouses at Piraeus, and Athens became the most cosmopolitan of all the Greek cities.

Athens' commercial prosperity aroused the enmity of its neighbours, chiefly Sparta. The Spartans feared that the Athenians and their allies (who formed the Delian League after the Persian Wars) would dominate them. The result was the Peloponnesian War from 431 to 404 BC. The first 10 years were indecisive; then a peace agreement supposed to last 50 years broke down within five. The Athenians failed to use their naval power effectively: a failed attempt to capture Sicily resulted in the loss of many Athenian ships, and the Spartans built a fleet of their own to cut off Athens' grain supplies. The Spartan leader Lysander allied himself with the Persians, and in 404 BC Athens was starved into surrender. The defeat of Athens meant the end of its 'Golden Age' and a Spartan-imposed oligarchy under the rule of the 'Thirty Tyrants'.

A bust of Pericles, now in the British Museum. At the end of the first year's campaigning in the Peloponnesian War, Pericles delivered a celebrated funeral oration for all those who had been killed, but he did not live to see the end of the war.

Horsemen from the Elgin Marbles. The sculptures on the Parthenon frieze from which the marbles come illustrate Greeks fighting Amazons, centaurs and Trojans, and gods battling giants. The frieze is thought by some experts to show elements of a great festival, the Panathenaia summer celebration in honour of the goddess Athena.

THE GODS LOOK DOWN

Athena was the patron goddess of Athens, enshrined within the Parthenon. Other cities venerated their own guardian deities and the Greek countryside was haunted by an assortment of supernatural beings (nymphs, centaurs, furies, satyrs, maenads, dryads and naiads).

The supreme gods and goddesses lived in palaces on Mount Olympus, the highest peak in Greece. Feasting on nectar and ambrosia, they gazed down on mortals. Their king was Zeus, the sky god who threw down thunderbolts to punish those mortals who offended him. Hera, wife of Zeus, with whom he was frequently at odds, controlled the weather, so farmers prayed to her – as did married women. Poseidon was the unruly god of the sea, earthquakes and horses, and Demeter (mother of Persephone) the goddess of grain and agriculture.

Athena, goddess of wisdom, was also the patron of spinning, weaving, pottery and other crafts. Aphrodite, goddess of love and fertility, born from the sea-foam, was married in a typical piece of Olympian mischief to Hephaestus, the lame and ill-favoured god of the forge.

A bust of Apollo, the sun god who, Greeks believed, drove his chariot across the sky every day.

Dionysus and supportive maenads (his female followers) painted on a red-figure kylix or drinking cup. The artist was Makron, c.490–480 BC.

The temple of Apollo at Delphi, on the southern slopes of Mount Parnassus, in the Pindus Mountains of central Greece.

People from all over Greece came to Delphi to consult the Delphic Oracle, the most famous oracle in the ancient world. The priestess, known as the Pythia, sat on a sacred tripod as she delivered Apollo's answers to questions in ambiguous terms. Each city-state maintained a treasury building at Delphi, where visiting citizens could deposit gifts for the gods.

Hermes, quick-witted messenger of the gods, with his winged sandals, was also god of trade and thieves. Apollo, the sun god, spoke through oracles and was also god of medicine, music, poetry and dance. Apollo's sister was Artemis, the huntress and goddess of childbirth. The Olympian pantheon was completed by Ares, god of war, and Hestia, goddess of the hearth – every town hall kept a fire burning in her honour.

Hades, brother of Zeus, ruled the Underworld. The Greeks thought heroes went to the Elysian Fields (which were heavenly), while lesser mortals crossed three rivers (Acheron, Lethe and Styx) to reside in a gloomy world where the dead wandered as 'shades'. At a funeral, relatives and friends made offerings of bowls of milk and bottles of blood, and left food and drink in the grave to accompany the dead person, along with honey cakes for Cerberus, the three-headed dog that guarded the Underworld. A coin was placed in the corpse's mouth to pay Charon, the ferryman who would take the body across the rivers.

Two important Athenian religious festivals were the Eleusinian Mysteries and the Dionysia. The Mysteries were nocturnal and secret. Honouring Demeter, they ensured a good harvest. The Dionysia spring festival celebrated Dionysus, a 'demi-god', who was a son of Zeus and a mortal mother. Dionysus taught mortals how to make wine. His festival involved a cheery procession and much drinking.

The Venus de Milo – perhaps the most famous of all statues from the ancient world. The marble statue, now on display in the Louvre Museum, Paris, is thought to depict Aphrodite (known as Venus by the Romans).

15

ART AND ARCHITECTURE

Wherever they settled, the Greeks built temples. Some temples were large, measuring over 60 metres (196 feet) by 110 metres (360 feet), though later in the Classical period such extravagance was thought vulgar. Many temples were small, since rituals and sacrifices normally took place at an open-air altar. Inside the temple itself, the cult-statue was lit only by light from the door or by torches.

A feature of Greek architecture is its use of fixed forms. Architects would use the diameter of a column as a base unit from which to calculate the proportions of an entire building and determine, for example, the number, height and spacing of columns. The Greek 'orders of architecture', a conventional system of columns (Doric, Ionic and Corinthian), were later adopted by the Romans and revived by European Renaissance architects.

Greek architects used stone as their ancestors had used timber for vertical columns and horizontal beams – the arch was known but seldom used. Stones were usually laid without mortar, kept in place by careful jointing and their own weight, supplemented by metal clamps and dowels. In a peristyle or colonnade, the columns were often load-bearing, but columns were also used purely for decorative effect.

Bronze charioteer from the Sanctuary of Apollo at Delphi. Dating from about 470 BC, the statue is one of the best preserved examples of Classical bronze sculpture; now in the Archaeological Museum of Delphi.

FIVE WONDERS OF THE ANCIENT WORLD

The Greeks created five of the Seven Wonders of the Ancient World.

The statue of Zeus at Olympia, built in 435 BC; fate unknown

The lighthouse at Alexandria, built 346 – 283 BC; collapsed in the 14th century

The Temple of Artemis at Ephesus, built c.550 BC; burned down in 356 BC

The Colossus of Rhodes, built c.210 BC; fell in an earthquake in 224 BC

The Mausoleum at Halicarnassus, built c.353 BC; fragments survive

Doric columns from the temple at Segesta, Sicily, built between 430 and 420 BC. Of the three orders, Doric is the most solid-looking and the simplest, more akin to the timber post that inspired it.

Ionic columns from the Erectheum in Athens. Ionic columns have a distinctive rolled-top decoration, or volute. The shaft of the column is channelled into flutes, typically 24 in an Ionic or Corinthian column.

Corinthian columns from the Temple of Olympian Zeus in Athens. Corinthian columns are more elaborate at the top than Doric or Ionic columns, with swirling acanthus leaves.

Roofs were usually wooden, with terracotta tiles. Mouldings and carvings on friezes or other decorative features were originally painted in bright colours, as were many statues.

Greek sculptors such as Phidias, Praxiteles, Lysippus and Myron created stunning lifelike figures combining idealism and naturalism. Many Classical statues did not survive the centuries. Much statuary was cast in bronze and suffered at the hands of later plunderers, who melted it down. Many Greek statues are now known only from copies that were made in later Greco-Roman or Roman times.

Few examples of Greek painting have survived outside tombs. Some of the best examples come from the royal tombs at Vergina in Macedonia. Similarly, later Greek painting is known chiefly from Roman copies, such as those at Pompeii. Far more plentiful is Greek painting on pottery, often in a vigorous, free style.

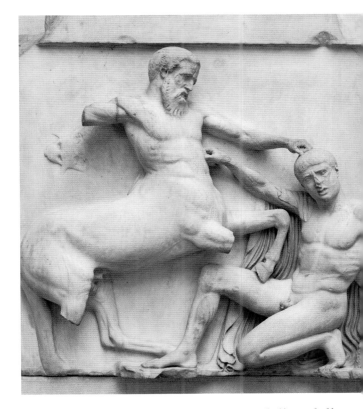

This portion of the Elgin Marbles shows a centaur (half man, half horse) fighting a Lapith – a legendary Greek from Thessaly. In mythology, Chiron the centaur was wise and skilled in medicine, but centaurs as a race were wild and uncivilized.

DAILY LIFE

Greek houses were built of stone, mud-bricks and timber, with a roof of clay tiles. Houses were constructed around courtyards, with doors leading to the rooms on the ground floor. A statue of the god Hermes by the front door served to ward off evil. Stairs from the courtyard led to the upper-floor bedrooms and servants' rooms. In winter, heating came from charcoal burned in metal braziers or from an open fire on the hearth.

The philosopher Plato (*c*.429–347 BC) advised men not to marry until their 30s, but brides were likely to be much younger. A suitable husband was usually chosen by a girl's father. Women in Athens could not inherit or own property. A married woman of middle class or higher rank did not often leave home, except for family parties or religious festivals. The richer the family, the less freedom a woman was likely to have. Some women, trained as hetaerae (companions) and adept at music and witty conversation, were invited to men-only gatherings, but normally men and women socialized separately.

A relief showing hydria (three-handled water pots) carriers, from the Parthenon frieze; now in the Acropolis Museum, Athens.

Head of a woman, said to be Aspasia of Miletus, from the 5th century BC. Aspasia was a powerful woman in Athens; she was the mother of Pericles' son, and frequently the target for satirists critical of her supposed influence.

An early 5th-century BC black-figure pot decorated with a scene of a shoemaker cutting leather for a shoe.

Jugs for water or wine, probably from Athens, made in the shape of heads: a maenad and a satyr; from 500–450 BC.

Wealthy women bathed most days, using perfumed oils. Many wore makeup, although it was fashionable to have pale skin rather than a suntan. Women wore tunic-style dresses, belted at the waist, and wraps when they went out. Men wore kilts or tunics fastened at the shoulder, and short cloaks if horse riding. Slaves and farmers toiling under a hot sun often wore little more than a loin cloth. Greek men cut their hair short and beards were trimmed or shaved off. Women had long hair, fastened with ribbons, metal bands or scarves. Men and women wore wide-brimmed hats to shade them from the sun, and usually wore leather sandals or walked barefoot.

Basic foods included porridge, bread, lentils, barley and beans. Breakfast was perhaps a piece of bread soaked in wine, and lunch might be bread and cheese with nuts, olives or figs. The evening meal might include goats' cheese, fish, vegetables (lettuce, cabbage, onions and leeks) with figs, grapes and honey. Meat was a luxury: it might be beef or mutton, with wild boar, venison or hare as a treat. Grapes were made into wine, and much of the olive crop was pressed for oil, used for cooking and as fuel in lamps. In Athens, it was a criminal offence to destroy an olive tree.

GREEK URNS

'When old age shall this generation waste, thou shalt remain,' wrote John Keats in his 'Ode on a Grecian Urn' (1820). The ravages of time destroy wood, metal, even stone – yet pottery survives even when smashed to pieces. The Greeks made pots in many forms: small jars and jugs, large amphorae, plates, drinking vessels, food bowls, mortars, lamps, perfume flasks, cosmetic boxes and chamber pots. Decorated pottery gives vivid insights into Greek life.

PLAYWRIGHTS AND PHILOSOPHERS

Greece was the first country where drama developed as a serious and popular art form, and Greek theatre reached new heights in Athens in the 400s BC. Though mythology was a powerful inspiration, playwrights explored themes central not just to Greek life but to all humanity: kinship, love, revenge, family, identity, honour and the relationship between men and gods.

Almost every Greek city had a theatre, with rows of seats in a semi-circle around a dance area (the *orchestra*). Facing the audience was the *skene* or stage house, which served as a backdrop and had doors through which actors could enter and exit. The actors were all men and all wore masks. Audiences of up to 15,000 watched the plays.

Hundreds of Greek tragedies were written, but only 33 survive, preserving for the modern audience works by the playwrights Aeschylus, Sophocles and Euripides. The only complete trilogy (the usual form of Greek tragedy) that survives is the *Oresteia* written by Aeschylus, which tells of the murder of Agamemnon by his wife Clytemnestra, her subsequent murder by her son Orestes, and his trial and acquittal. Sophocles is perhaps the closest to a modern dramatist in his construction of character and plot; many critics think his *Oedipus Rex* the greatest Greek drama we have.

Euripides, one of the three greatest tragedians of Classical Athens, holding an actor's mask.

MINOAN SCRIPT

The earliest Greek writing comes from Crete. British archaeologist Sir Arthur Evans (1851–1941), who began excavating the Palace of Knossos in the 1890s, found 3,000 clay tablets inscribed with writing, now known as Linear A and Linear B. Similar tablets with Linear B script were found at Thebes and Mycenae. Not until 1952 were the scripts deciphered. Most (though not all) scholars accept the writing as a form of Greek. It shows that the Cretans made lists – of slave women, sheep, pigs, goats, bronze vessels and oil – as befitted a trading people.

The theatre at Epidaurus, Greece, designed by Polykleitos the Younger in the 4th century BC.

This terracotta actor's mask shows a slave-character, from the 2nd century BC.

Comedies were usually satirical, making fun of prominent citizens and events of the day. Eleven comedies by Aristophanes (a stern critic of the contemporary scene) survive, and just one by a later writer, Menander, who depends for his laughs far more on plotted coincidences and private goings-on.

The three greatest philosophers of the ancient world were Greek: Socrates, Plato and Aristotle. Socrates left no writings, but his pupil Plato left an account of his ideas, set out in the form of dialogues between teacher and pupil. Plato lectured at a school in Athens and one of his pupils was Aristotle, whose interests were universal, and who in turn founded his own school, the Lyceum.

The Greek philosophers ranged widely across the intellectual spectrum: Zeno of Citium founded Stoicism; Epicurus taught that the aim of life is pleasure (though not all pleasure is good); Pyrrho, the Sceptic, believed that our senses only deceive us; and Diogenes, the Cynic, reputedly lived in a barrel and told Alexander the Great to stand aside because he was blocking out the sunlight.

Stone bust of Plato, founder of the Academy in Athens, where Aristotle studied.

THE OLYMPIC GAMES

The restored stadium at Olympia, dating from the 5th century BC, home of the first Olympics.

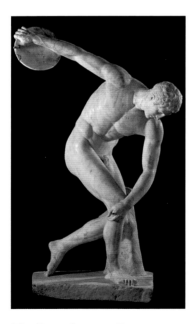

The discus-thrower, a Roman copy of a 5th-century BC statue attributed to Myron. The discus was made of marble or metal; various weights of discus have been found, but how far Greek athletes could hurl them is not known.

Every four years, people from all over Greece assembled for the Olympic Games, in one of the earliest and longest lasting demonstrations of 'pan-Hellenism'. Greece was not an easy country for travellers. The interior was mountainous and there were few roads better than rough tracks. Wealthy people rode horses, while merchants used mules and donkeys as pack animals; farmers drove carts pulled by horses or oxen. Hotels were used by important travellers only, most people staying with relatives or friends, or at inns. In towns, strangers bedded down on the porches of public buildings. The sea was the easiest way for many to reach the Games, which were staged on a flat plain at Olympia in western Greece.

The Olympic Games were held in honour of Zeus. The earliest record of them is from 776 BC, and they continued every four years until the AD 390s. Almost as important as the Olympic Games were the Isthmian, Nemean and Pythian games. The Pythian Games, held at Delphi, included music and singing.

The Olympic Games lasted for five days, with the final day given over to victory celebrations. Winners earned great prestige as well as a crown of olive leaves, and poems were composed in their praise. A Greek city whose athletes did well enhanced its reputation.

Olympic competitors had to be men and Greek by language or descent; athletes competed naked and women were not allowed to watch, unless they were priestesses. Athletes trained at their city's gymnasium, which had a wrestling ground, running tracks, baths and rooms used for lectures and for oiling and massaging aching muscles. At the Olympics, all events were for individual athletes. The only event in the first 13 Olympic Games was a running race called the *stadion*, over a distance of 192 metres (210 yards). Over subsequent years, other events were added, including boxing, a vicious form of all-in wrestling that included kicking, the long jump, javelin, discus, horse and chariot racing, and the pentathlon. The pentathlon's five events were running, wrestling, discus, long jump and javelin. There were unusual competitions, too, such as races for chariots pulled by two mules and a race between warriors wearing full armour.

The first recorded Olympic winner was Koroibos, a cook from Elis. The all-time champion was Milo of Kroton, who won five wrestling events between 536 and 520 BC, and is said to have carried an ox on his shoulders around the stadium at Olympia on his final appearance.

CRACKING DOWN ON CHEATS

Bronze statues of Zeus were erected with the proceeds from fines imposed on cheats at the Olympic Games. The first person to be so fined was a man named Empolis, from Thessaly. During the 98th Olympic Games in 398 BC, he was found guilty of bribing boxers.

Black-figure amphora showing athletes racing.

Bronze statuette of a horseman dismounting. Greeks liked horse racing, a dangerous sport when riders rode bare-back.

ALEXANDER THE GREAT

In the 300s BC, freed from the fear of Persian invasion, the leading Greek city-states (Athens, Sparta and Thebes) quarrelled and fought for supremacy until unity was imposed on them. The iron fist was that of Philip II of Macedonia and the grand vision was that of his son, Alexander.

Alexander, a teenage student of Aristotle, was leading armies in battle at the age of 16. After his father was assassinated in 336 BC, he swiftly eliminated all rivals at home, routed any opposition in Greece (razing Thebes, for example) and then marched off to attack Persia. His victory at the Battle of Issus (in modern Turkey) in 333 BC put King Darius to flight. Next, Alexander proceeded south to Egypt, where he consulted the oracle at Siwah and was crowned pharaoh. He then turned on Mesopotamia, defeating Darius again at Gaugamela and occupying Babylon and Persepolis. By 327 BC, the conqueror was in northeast India, fighting King Porus.

Marble head of Alexander the Great; now in the British Museum.

Alexander the Great, at the Battle of Issus; from the 1st-century BC 'Alexander Mosaic' originally in the House of the Faun at Pompeii, Italy.

Though Alexander himself dreamed of a fusion of cultures (Greek, Persian, Egyptian, Babylonian), Greek ways took root in the lands through which he passed, creating a vast Hellenistic (Greek-style) empire. When he finally headed back west, his exhausted army endured a nightmarish desert trek through Baluchistan (Pakistan). Recovering in Babylon and busy with new imperial plans, Alexander died – reportedly after a bout of heavy drinking, in 323 BC. He had been king for almost 12 years and was not yet 33.

None of Alexander's successors was strong enough to hold his empire together. It fractured. Ptolemy, one of Alexander's generals, had Alexander's body brought to Alexandria for burial. His successor, Ptolemy II, established Alexandria's library and the city drew in intellectuals and scientists from all over the Mediterranean world. Queen Cleopatra (died 31 BC) was the last of the Ptolemy line to rule Egypt. Another Greek general, Seleukos, founded the Seleucid dynasty with its capital at Antioch (Turkey).

A bronze cavalryman's helmet, from Boeotia, of the kind worn by Alexander's crack cavalry force.

ALEXANDER'S ARMY

The Greek infantry soldier, or hoplite, carried a long spear, a short sword and a large round shield. The infantry advanced in formation, known as the phalanx. In the time of Alexander the Great, the phalanx became huge: 1,500 men in 15 ranks, each man wielding a spear 6 metres (20 feet) long. This armoured mass, bristling with spearpoints, simply bulldozed its way through the enemy. Alexander added a superb cavalry force, the Companions, which he often led in person, mounted on his favourite horse, Bucephalus.

A gold casket from the tomb of Alexander's father, Philip II. It is decorated with the 16-ray star emblem of the Macedonian royal dynasty.

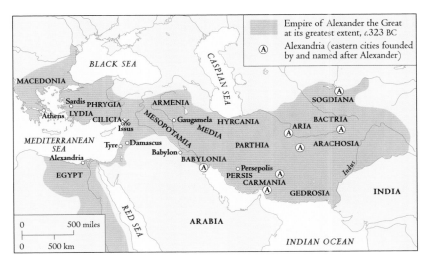

This map shows the vast empire conquered by Alexander the Great.

THE GREEK GENIUS

When Greece passed under the control of Rome in the 140s BC, the Romans were impressed by, even in awe of, Greek cultural achievements, although they were often acerbic about Greeks themselves. They adopted Greek gods and myths, studied Greek philosophy and science and copied Greek architecture and art. Intellectual inquiry flourished, especially at Alexandria, and the Hellenistic world became as notable for its ideas as for its architecture, commerce and military expertise.

Remarkable evidence of that ingenuity still comes to light. The Antikythera Mechanism, a bronze calculating machine salvaged in fragments from a Roman shipwreck in 1901, and now reconstructed, was the earliest known mechanism with a system of gear-wheels. Made in the 2nd century BC, it was used to determine the motions of the Sun and Moon, and as a prototype 'computer' was unmatched in complexity until the first mechanical clocks, almost 1,500 years later.

The Antikythera Mechanism, time-worn after almost 2,500 years, but a remarkable insight into Greek ingenuity.

The Romans were greatly influenced by Greek architecture, so that 'Greco-Roman style' was often seamless. This is the Roman entrance to the agora (marketplace) at Ephesus (modern Turkey), which was originally built in the Hellenistic period.

Aristotle (384–322 BC); born in Stagira, northeast Greece, he was one of the most influential philosophers in the history of Western thought.

Greek engineering was usually small-scale, although their generals became masters of siege craft, using catapults, mines, siege towers and battering rams. Hero of Alexandria built the first steam turbine (as a toy), but the Greeks had little need of large machinery: slaves and animals did the heavy work in their world. Yet their interest in pure science – in atoms, stars, forces, motion, geometry – and their love of gadgets (even ones as impractical as the feathery wings of the legendary Daedalus and Icarus) laid the foundation for later technologies. Aristotle, regarded as the starting point for science until the Middle Ages, and Ptolemy, whose world-view shaped the maps of later geographers, dominated Western thought until the revelations of Copernicus, Galileo and Newton in the 16th and 17th centuries.

It appears some Greeks were early environmentalists, too. Solon suggested banning the ploughing of hillsides to prevent soil erosion, while Plato lamented that 'there are some mountains that have nothing but food for bees, but they had trees not long ago.'

Pythagoras (580–500 BC) said 'everything is numbers.' Right-angled triangles were not his sole concern. He believed in metempsychosis – the passage of souls between bodies (human to human, human to animal).

EUREKA!

Greek scientists and mathematicians were hugely influential. Euclid's *Elements* was the standard geometry text for 2,000 years, while Pythagoras explained the right-angled triangle for the benefit of later generations (including generations of schoolchildren). Democritus was the first to suggest the theory of atoms, while the astronomer Hipparchus worked out the length of a year to within 6.5 minutes. Archimedes (whether in the bath or not) established principles of hydrostatics used by physicists ever since. Hippocrates, known as the 'father of medicine', taught that disease was best diagnosed by examination of the body.

Archimedes (c.280–211/212 BC), the most famous Greek inventor and mathematician. He was born, and died, in Italy, at the colony city-state of Syracuse.

THE GREEK INHERITANCE

Renaissance artists reinterpreted Greek myths; the Italian artist Benvenuto Cellini (1500–71) shows Perseus with the head of the gorgon Medusa on this statue in Florence.

After the fall of the western Roman Empire in AD 476, many Greek manuscripts from Roman libraries were lost or scattered across Europe and the Middle East. Many lost works are now known only by their titles. Yet Greek ideas survived in both the Christian and Islamic worlds during the European 'dark ages' and were rediscovered during the Renaissance (1400s–1500s).

Homer influenced the Roman poet Virgil, and both were imitated by later writers such as Milton. Dramatists in 17th-century France wrote plays that strictly observed Greek rules (the 'unities' of time, place and action).

The façade of the British Museum in London, with its Ionic-style columns. The building was designed in the 1820s in the 'Greek Revival' style but it was not finished until 1852.

Sculptors studied Greek statues (often from Roman copies); and the 18th century saw a 'neo-classical' revival when architects reinterpreted Greek forms in buildings and decoration. Interest in things Greek increased as rich Europeans did the 'grand tour' of ancient sites. The founding fathers of the United States saw Athenian democracy as a model for their new republic.

Long after ancient Greece lost its power, the extent of its influence is still immeasurable – on art, literature, architecture, political systems, philosophy and the history of science. Ancient Greece remains a potent ideal, visible through the ruins and museum objects that remain, and accessible through the words of the Greeks themselves. New discoveries are still made, as archaeologists research sites afresh. The tragedies of Sophocles, Aeschylus, Euripides and the comedies of Aristophanes still provide inspiration for modern playwrights and move audiences as they did over 2,000 years ago.

Erasistratus of Cos (3rd century BC) identified the heart as the motor of the circulation system. Ancient Greece was in many ways the heart, and motor, of Western civilization.